M000031329

Published by Standard Publishing, Cincinnati, Ohio
www.standardpub.com

Copyright © 2007 by CHRIST IN YOUTH

Project editor: Kelly Carr
Cover and interior design: The DesignWorks Group
Printed in: China

ISBN 978-0-7847-2191-9

13 12 11 10 09 08 07   9 8 7 6 5 4 3 2 1

IT'S JUST BEGINNING

Is your mind swirling yet? Your emotions might be run ragged as you return home from your mission trip.

It's hard coming back. You anticipated the trip for so long. You experienced service like never before. You grew to love people from cultures and situations much different from your own. Then it was over. You said good-bye. You are now back in familiar surroundings, reflecting on your journey. It's kind of a letdown.

How do you process all that you learned from your time of service? God used you to spread his love, and during that time you grew into a stronger disciple for him. What does that mean for you now that you're home? Will your mission trip change you for the rest of your life?

It should. Because your journey didn't just end. Actually, it's just beginning.

REFLECT

To help you gather your thoughts and move forward, take these next fifteen days and reflect on your trip:

- How did it feel to get your hands dirty?

- What was it like to meet people who live with fewer possessions and privileges than you have?

- How did it feel to serve other people while you gained nothing for yourself?

- Remember the moments when your heart pumped rapidly in your chest while God provided just the right words for you to share Jesus with someone you met?

This book has fifteen devotions and journaling space to help you reflect on your mission trip. Think about the insight you gained from seeing God's love for people in all walks of life. Consider what you will do now to continue living out the service you participated in on your trip.

These devotions were written by people who have served the Lord both in the U.S. and in places beyond. They share what God has taught them in order to help you listen for the Holy Spirit to speak to you as you continue to serve God back home.

Reflect on the transformation God has made in your life. Reflect on who you are now and what more you can do for his kingdom.

WHAT GOD STARTED

by Mike Schrage

Just what has God begun in you? Through your mission trip, God has started something in you, and the one "who was, and is, and is to come" (Revelation 4:8) is able to complete what he started. God is not a quitter. God is a master creator, a craftsman, and an ultimate can-do God. There is none like him.

CHOSEN AND BLESSED

Genesis tells us that we are created "in the image of God" (Genesis 1:27). God, the image maker! Thousands of years later, the prophet Isaiah promised that God would do "a new thing" so impossible it would be like creating a cool stream in a hot desert (Isaiah 43:18, 19). God, the inventor! Then the message continued centuries later in the Ephesian letter when Paul stated that you and I were "created in Christ Jesus to do good works" (Ephesians 2:10). God, the implementer!

You are uniquely designed, especially prepared, and ultimately called to do tasks for the living God. These tasks might not always be special; sometimes you might simply be doing mundane things in extraordinary ways!

You have heard the name of Jesus, you have accepted him into your life and have been filled with the Holy Spirit, and you have now experienced God by serving him through a mission trip. You are chosen and blessed—blessed to go, blessed to give, and blessed to gain and seek more fame and glory for him!

God is working through people around the world because he desires and plans for people from every tribe, tongue, and nation to worship him (Revelation 7:9). This worship will fit together like pieces in the giant jigsaw puzzle of God's grand plan.

He is creating a new masterpiece once again after Adam and Eve allowed Satan to break and trash the first fantastic art treasure known as the Garden of Eden. "A new heaven and a new earth" await us (2 Peter 3:13; Revelation 21:1). Aren't you excited?! We can add to the masterpiece when we tell others how they too can join God in Heaven.

TENSION

You have experienced a taste of tension these past few weeks. Life can be easy, life can be hard, and life can be assumed to be hard when it's really easy! That is the rub in your heart this week.

Before your trip, your wealth might have been taken for granted and squandered like sand through the fingers. You may have simply expected health, but then all around you on the mission trip there were signs of sickness. You saw hope placed in things instead of in the maker of those things. And in the process of this tension, a new community of worshipers developed on your journey as you worked together with others and served cross-culturally.

Tuck the tension deep into your heart. Let it be used by God to sharpen your spiritual sense of justice, equity, and holiness. Pain can be good. Let the spiritual struggle and pain come as a special guest into your heart, and let God mold it to be more like Christ's heart.

God is a confident God because he knows his plan and is working his plan through you! Just because you left your mission trip location does not mean God has left those you met there! And he has not left you to simply return to life as usual.

You might ask, "What can I do now? I'm not special." If by "special" you mean that you are not a super speaker or leader like some TV preacher or the announcing angel Gabriel—you're right! However, God says you are part of "a chosen people, a royal priesthood, a holy nation, a people belonging to God, that you may declare the praises of him who called you out of darkness into his wonderful light" (1 Peter 2:9).

Royal—so that you can help lift up the helpless commoner. Holy—so you can permeate the unholy crevasses of life. And most of all, chosen by God—to help his causes, purposes, and people. So feel special now, and realize that you have a job to do!

You may not be called to China as a full-time missionary, but you are called to love your family and neighbors. You may not be asked to go to the inner city of Chicago, but you are asked to give kindness to others. You may never be required to suffer for Jesus or die as a martyr. On the other hand, you might be called to do these things! But no matter what you do, you are required to obey!

But you say, "It's hard." You're right. Life is hard and messy. But remember that "the one who is in you is greater than the one who is in the world" (1 John 4:4). As God lives in you, he wants to use you just as you are, right where you live.

The story is told in 2 Kings 5 of Naaman, the army commander who suffered from leprosy. He visited Elisha, the prophet, who told Naaman to wash himself in the Jordan River. Naaman stomped away in disgust. The servants of Naaman reasoned with the commander for a moment and stated that if the prophet of God had asked him to do a hard thing, he would have gladly done it to get rid of his leprosy. They basically told Naaman, "Look, he is simply asking you to do a common thing. So do it, and be healed!" Naaman obeyed and was healed.

How many times are we like Naaman when God asks us to do something simple? *If God would ask me to do some important task, I'd gladly do it*, we tell ourselves. *But to take out the trash, to serve my siblings, and to bite my tongue when I want to lash out at someone who has wronged me—that's hard.*

The day-to-day small acts can be hard, but they are simple things we can all do—like Naaman did when he went to the Jordan River. God asks us to do the common, ordinary things in extraordinarily good fashion. Doing even the simple things gives the credit to God and not to people, and that is always God's agenda.

COMPLETION

So whether you're in Liberia or your living room, God can complete what he has started in your heart during your mission trip—if you'll trust and obey.

What has God started in you? Will you let God carry out his plan through your life?

Thank God for the tension and messy feelings in your heart that happened because of your mission trip. Ask God to use that tension to build trust and confidence in how he wants to work through you now that you have returned. Promise to give God the honor and glory in the daily moments of your life.

My Reflection

_____

_____

_____

_____

_____

_____

_____

_____

_____

_____

_____

_____

_____

_____

_____

_____

A LETTER FROM BROOKE

by Bill Baumgardner

The following is a letter from a teen who served on a Know Sweat service project team organized by Christ in Youth (CIY). She wrote to tell CIY what she gained from serving others in a different part of the U.S.

THE OUTREACH CENTER

"Hi, my name is Brooke, and I'm from Missouri. I want to thank you all at CIY for what you do. It's amazing! Coming home from Cincinnati, Ohio, I thought over my whole week—the fights, the touching moments, and so on. But what really stuck in my mind was my time spent with an old woman.

"We arrived at our work area, an outreach center, early Tuesday morning; none of us really knew what to expect. As we walked in, one of the most amazing women I have ever met came out to greet us; but the greetings were short. There was work to be done!

"The first thing the outreach center did was sign us up to shadow volunteers who regularly worked there. The volunteers were to teach us our jobs and show us exactly what this place, Outreach, did. I signed up to work in the Wellness Center, where I would soon learn that medicine was given away. More importantly, all expired medications had to be thrown out. So most of my time was spent dating bottle after bottle and box after box of medicine.

"But during open hours, I interacted with people from the neighborhood. I talked to young moms with no teeth; I met people who told me about past drug addictions, alcohol abuse, and abusive relationships; and I saw children who smelled horrible, begging stuff so they could live. It was definitely humbling."

A WOMAN OF JOY

"But the person who sticks out the most in my mind was an old lady; I never got her name, but that doesn't really matter. We all served her food, clothing, medication, etc. But she served us more than we could ever realize. This hunchbacked, thin, sweet lady came in to get some medicine for her sore joints. While someone went back to get her stuff, I stayed and talked to her.

"She was so excited because her church was taking her on a trip. She was leaving the thirteenth and coming back on the fifteenth. You want to know how I know? Because she was so enthusiastic about it, I must have heard it three hundred times! Soon she left, and we began to shut down the center.

"A few minutes later, John, our leader, poked his head in and asked if I would like to join him. I climbed in the van with this family of dirty children who wouldn't stop crying for their mom. John went to get groceries; but when he came back, he not only had groceries but also that old woman. First, we went to her house, which was in horrible condition, and dropped her and the groceries off.

"Everyone, including the young children, got out and helped. Before we left, John asked if it was all right to say a prayer. You could tell she was a little uncomfortable, but she let him. He took her frail hands in his and began to pray. That prayer was nothing special, but then she turned around and I could see her face. Her face was full of light, joy, and compassion. Her eyes brimmed with tears. She turned back to John with tears streaming down her cheeks and gave him a hug and thanked him. Then she turned to me, still crying, and hugged me and told me to never forget her. I promised I wouldn't.

"That small, frail woman touched me in a way I didn't think was possible. That week God sent me to serve others and to change myself."

BLESSED BY LOVING OTHERS

Perhaps you have a story similar to Brooke's. Who touched your life during your mission trip? How can the memory of such a person spur you on to serve people in your own community?

God's love is amazing. It's so incredible that *we* receive a blessing when we love and serve others. Remind yourself of the importance God places on love by reading 1 Corinthians 13. Pray that God will help you to love and serve the people whom he places in your daily life.

My Reflection

My Reflection

_____

_____

_____

_____

_____

_____

_____

_____

_____

_____

_____

_____

_____

_____

_____

BE PART OF THE SOLUTION

by Matt Gilchrist

There is a big difference between people who talk about a problem and people who do something about it. For a number of years, I was a youth minister. One of the most draining things about my time in ministry was when people complained about a situation but never would do anything about it.

"We need more programs for our kids" or "There aren't enough good teachers" or "Why are these facilities so run down?" Over and over, people complained to me or criticized something. But when the challenge was given for them to be a part of the solution, they disappeared into the woodwork.

On your mission trip, you were challenged to look around you and see needs you could meet. You were challenged to be a person who doesn't just see a need but a person who responds to that need. That same challenge is now set before you as you are back home.

NEHEMIAH AND THE BROKEN WALLS

Nehemiah was a man who didn't just see a need but someone who got busy being part of the solution. Nehemiah was a part of the Israelite nation that was in captivity, but his life was blessed. He lived in a palace in Persia, serving as the cupbearer for King Artaxerxes. So he had the rare privilege of being able to speak face-to-face with the leader of a country.

While Nehemiah and the Israelites were in exile, their treasured city of Jerusalem, home to God's temple, was destroyed. Stories about how Jerusalem was lying in ruins slowly made their way to Persia. Nehemiah heard these stories and was moved to do something. More than simply being upset about it or wishing someone would do something, Nehemiah took it upon himself to rebuild the walls around Jerusalem and return it to a city of strength (Nehemiah 1).

When the king noticed Nehemiah's sadness, Nehemiah boldly asked to return to his homeland to rebuild the walls. King Artaxerxes actually agreed, and Nehemiah left with the king's blessing (Nehemiah 2).

I'm amazed at the boldness of Nehemiah, and I'm inspired that when he saw a need, he sought God in prayer (1:5-11) and then acted.

But it wasn't easy. Nehemiah and his people faced opposition (Nehemiah 4). So Nehemiah created a game plan in which some people built while others defended (vv. 16-18).

We even read that the people worked with one hand and carried a weapon with the other! In the end, the walls were rebuilt in just fifty-two days, despite all the resistance!

When the walls of Jerusalem were complete, even those who had tried to stop the process realized that the work was done because of God's help—the ultimate compliment to a job well done!

Here are some lessons we can learn from Nehemiah:

WALK WITH GOD

Throughout the book of Nehemiah, we read over and over again about him praying. Look through the first six chapters and mark all the times Nehemiah prays or calls to God.

When Nehemiah faced opposition he always seemed to know what to do. Nothing seemed to discourage or cripple his vision. What was his secret? No matter what the situation was, Nehemiah kept going because he knew God was with him.

When you see a need, are you more likely to just jump in, or do you stop and pray? How do you react when you face opposition?

DON'T GET TOO COMFORTABLE

Nehemiah had it pretty good, under the circumstances. Sure his country was in exile because the people had made God upset. But he was working in a palace; he got good meals, he had a nice place to sleep, and his life wasn't in grave danger every moment. But he gave all that up and put his life on the line to rebuild the walls of Jerusalem and, by doing so, to strengthen God's people.

God probably used your mission trip to open your eyes in many ways. What did you learn about the suffering or struggles of others that you didn't know before the trip? What are some things you can do to step out of your comfort zone in order to reach out to struggling people?

Think about people around you who are in crisis. What can you do to help them, even if it means sacrificing some of your personal comfort? Remember, God can use small sacrifices to do great things. For example, perhaps you have a family member who recently went through a divorce. Taking the family a meal or mowing their yard could free up the newly single parent to have quality time with the kids one evening.

REVIVE OTHERS

God woke up the nation of Israel through Nehemiah and his mission to rebuild the walls. Nehemiah was faithful, and as a result the people of Israel remembered who they were and what they had done wrong and began to do the right thing again. This revival happened through work. Imagine starting a revival in the hearts of those around you through the work that you do.

Why do you think people respond so strongly to seeing faith in action? In what ways can you use actions to revive your family? your church? your school? your community?

DON'T JUST TALK—GET MOVING!

"God can't steer you if you aren't moving." My friend who is a missionary pilot in Africa said those words to me when we were on a mission trip. He reminded me that he can turn the wheel of his airplane all he wants, but unless there is forward momentum, the plane won't go anywhere.

My friend's challenge to me is my challenge to you: start moving. Start doing what you think God is calling you to, and if he wants to change the direction, he will. But he can't change your direction when you are just sitting there. Don't be one of those people who complain about the problems but won't be a part of the solution.

What do you feel God calling you to do now that you are back home from your mission trip?

A PERSON OF ACTION

My prayer for you is that when you see a need you'll ask God for guidance and then do whatever is necessary to take action. You will face opposition as you try to do God's will for your life—not everyone will be excited about what you are doing. But when you work in God's name, with his power, things will get done that you never would have imagined, and it will be evident to others how God used you.

Take some time to ask God to help you be a person of action. Ask him to show you the things you need to do. Nehemiah was a man who left the comforts of his life to do something huge for God. Pray for that same attitude and the strength to live it out.

My Reflection

ALL OUR STUFF

by Wade Landers

Look at the following list and check off the things your family has:

- ❑ food (even extra in the cabinets)
- ❑ clothes (more than a week's worth)
- ❑ a place to live
- ❑ furniture
- ❑ running water
- ❑ electricity
- ❑ heat
- ❑ air-conditioning
- ❑ stove
- ❑ microwave
- ❑ one or more phones
- ❑ CD player/MP3 player

- ❑ DVD player
- ❑ computer
- ❑ Internet service
- ❑ one or more TVs
- ❑ one or more cars
- ❑ cable or satellite

If you checked off more than eleven items, you are in one of the richest families in the world! When you look at how much stuff Americans typically have, it is mind-boggling. And it begs the question, what are we doing with all our stuff?

"Watch out! Be on your guard against all kinds of greed; a man's life does not consist in the abundance of his possessions" (Luke 12:15). These are the words of Jesus—and they are tough to hear, especially when you look at the world around us. Consider these statistics estimated by various sources: about three billion people live on less than two dollars per day; up to a billion people worldwide live in slums; approximately thirty thousand children die every day from hunger and poverty-related diseases; and sadly, Americans spend over a hundred billion dollars annually on fast food!

IS IT WRONG TO HAVE THINGS?

Are you greedy? Does your life consist in the abundance of the things you have? If I came by your house, stepped into your bedroom, looked around, and searched in your closet, in your dresser drawers, under the bed . . . what would I find?

Read Luke 12:13-21, 32-34. Write down anything you feel the Holy Spirit is telling you through these Scriptures.

So is it wrong to have so much stuff? That's a tough question because the answer could be yes and could be no. You will have to decide. Is your life tangled up in things? Do you measure how good life is by the stuff you get? Do you think things will make you happy?

Think about the people you saw on your mission trip. You probably observed those who had much less than you. What do they really need?

ACTION STEPS

If life is truly about God's kingdom and a relationship with Jesus, and you were to fully live out that purpose, what would you change about the stuff you have? What are some action steps you can consider now that you are home?

I have a few ideas for you!

1. Give away some stuff. Clean out your closet. Declutter. Be OK with a lot less. Tithe—give God a portion of your money. Remember, it's his anyway.

2. Consider fasting once a week. Food can have just as powerful a hold on us as items such as clothes and video games.

3. Support a missionary. Sponsor a child in a poor country. Anything that makes you give up something you want so others can have what they need. Consider volunteering your time at a soup kitchen or food pantry.

4. Get organized. We can waste so much time that we end up not being able to do the very things we want to do! Clean out, throw away, and schedule your time so you can say yes to important things and no to lots of things that don't matter.

THE LIFE YOU WERE MEANT TO LIVE

Your things can keep you from living the life you were meant to live. Your things can keep you from God's mission field. Your things can keep you from growing in your spiritual walk. I am convinced that your things can keep you from God.

I challenge you to spend some time in prayer. Tell God you want your life to be about him and the things he cares about, not about stuff you want. Confess the times when you chose things you wanted rather than stopping to seek what God wanted. Thank God for the wealth he has given you and your family. Ask him for wisdom in how you can use what he has given you to further his kingdom. Thank God for getting your attention on your mission trip. Commit to live a life that points people toward him.

My Reflection

My Reflection

TREASURE

by Pat Fancher

As newlyweds, my husband and I lived in a tiny studio apartment directly across the street from American University in Washington, D.C. We owned five pieces of furniture—and the two cardboard end tables did not count!

Four years later, we had accumulated rooms of stuff. My husband was off to grad school, so we were headed to Fayetteville, Arkansas.

The movers carefully packed and loaded all our worldly possessions in the large moving van. Two weeks later, we received a message: "Our company regrets to inform you that the vehicle carrying your belongings wrecked on a mountain in West Virginia. Most of your furniture and other items were destroyed."

Shattered on that rugged mountainside was baby furniture my father had lovingly made for his first grandchild before he died of cancer. Irreplaceable items. Numb with shock, we tried to digest the devastating news.

Then tragedy quickly struck again. I started hemorrhaging, and the baby we were expecting died. Nothing can prepare you for such loss. Grief breaks open your heart, and your life is changed forever. We quickly learned that earthly possessions can be replaced—and that even treasured possessions aren't as valuable as people. Our baby could not be restored.

If we yield our lives to Christ, he heals our broken hearts, and out of suffering comes new beginnings. There is joy that lies ahead. I know. Just before Christmas the year after our tragedy, God blessed us with a sweet baby boy.

ETERNAL INVESTMENT

"Do not store up for yourselves treasures on earth, where moth and rust destroy, and where thieves break in and steal. But store up for yourselves treasures in heaven, where moth and rust do not destroy, and where thieves do not break in and steal. For where your treasure is, there your heart will be also" (Matthew 6:19-21).

Whatever controls your heart and soul will define what you do with your life. If you allow the standards of the world into your heart, you risk joining the ranks of those obsessed with material things. A population consumed with the shop-till-you-drop mentality that puts extreme emphasis on wealth, possessions, beauty, popularity, and perfection sets you up for failure and emptiness. Jesus warns us that the things of this world are temporary and do not satisfy.

In essence, Jesus teaches us that real happiness does not come from collecting wealth and possessions. Rather, he tells us to treasure the kingdom of God and to invest our lives in eternal ways.

In Luke 18:18-23, Jesus met a rich young ruler. The man had great wealth. The fact of having it was not his sin; the problem was cherishing it above eternal life. Jesus told him to sell everything and give it away to the poor so that he would have riches in Heaven. And then, Jesus said, "Come, follow me." Yet the man became sad because he did not want to give up his wealth.

Read Acts 4:36, 37. Barnabas also had great wealth, but he sold his estate and took the money to the apostles to be used for God.

After reading these Scriptures, can you think of material things that you value more than you should?

HEAVENLY JOY

Some of the happiest people I've met have no wealth at all. They are dirt poor. Serving in the dark corners of inner cities, I have met homeless people who are joy-filled despite their environment, simply because they have Jesus Christ in their hearts.

Think of the people you met and served on your mission trip. What did you learn about possessions from their lives? Which people appeared to have their focus on heavenly treasures rather than on earthly things?

The body of David Livingstone was buried in England where he was born, but at his request his heart was buried in Africa, the continent he loved. At the foot of a tall tree in a small African village, the natives dug a hole and placed in it the heart of this man they loved and respected.

If your heart were to be buried in the place you loved most during your life, where would it be? In your home? At your workplace? In your car? Where is your heart?

Examine your daily life. Do you have a healthy attitude toward material possessions? Is your heart treasuring godly things or earthly things?

Spend some time praying that the Holy Spirit to rid you of every selfish attitude in your heart and to empower you with righteousness. Ask God to help you use your possessions wisely so that you might bring him glory and honor.

My Reflection

My Reflection

EYES OF COMPASSION

by Bill Baumgardner

Caleb is the younger of my two teenage sons. He is a very compassionate person. Throughout his life he has shown me what it is to see with the eyes of Christ, to see with compassion.

One spring we were in Mexico doing preparation for a future mission trip. While I was checking out the work site, Caleb was out goofing around. Later that day when we were at the store, he was pleading for money from me. (He does that very well too!) Finally I asked him what he wanted money for, and he promptly told me it was to buy a soccer ball.

I proceeded to lecture Caleb about how he already had five soccer balls at home that he didn't play with and that he spent way too much money on junk. I went on and on. Then he explained, "Dad, it's not for me. It's for the kids at the home we visited." He said that if I had seen what the children were playing with, I would want to get them a soccer ball. The ball they were playing with had no insides. As a matter of fact, it was a piece of leather stuffed with grass! Needless to say, I gave him the money.

Just the other day, Caleb again wandered off from my wife and me when we were at the store. We didn't find him until we reached the parking lot. There was a lady in a wheelchair, and Caleb was loading her groceries into her car. He had seen her distress and reached out to help her.

GOD'S COMPASSION FOR US

I am humbled that my son has the eyes

to see people in need all around him and the compassion to serve them.

The compassion God has for us is overwhelming. Do a search in your Bible's concordance or online, and see how many times in the entire Bible God is described as having compassion for us, the flawed human beings he created. Start here by reading a few of these compassionate descriptions in the book of Psalms: Psalm 103:8, 13; Psalm 111:4; Psalm 116:5; Psalm 145:8, 9.

With God's great compassion for us, how can we not be compassionate for others—just as Caleb has already figured out?

COMPASSION FOR YOUR NEIGHBOR

I have also seen compassion shown through the teams I have led on service projects. One of my favorite service project areas is Cincinnati, Ohio. Each summer, youth groups from across the country go to Cincinnati to assist local outreach programs. One of the things we regularly do is serve meals in a downtown park to people who are homeless.

Many of the people who are homeless ask the teens, "Why?" I heard one student quickly respond, "Jesus told me to love my neighbor, and you are my neighbor." That particular student lived hundreds of miles away from Cincinnati, yet he understood God's command (Leviticus 19:18; Matthew 22:35-40) and saw the people as his neighbors.

I see other students choose to give up their boxed lunches. They know their next meal will be that evening, while those in the park might not eat again until the following week. For those students, compassion is not only a lesson they learned in Sunday school; it's also a lesson they put into practice.

Unfortunately, the inner city gets a bad name, but there are a lot of hurting people who need physical help, as well as needing the love of God shown to them. My guess is that no matter where you live, there is a "bad" section of town. And there are also people that need to be shown the love of Christ. I challenge you to gather some people from your church and find a safe way to serve those people.

COMPASSION FOR THOSE IN NEED

When you were on your mission trip, it was probably easy to see people in need. After all, you went to a specific location *because* people there had needs. But there are just as many people in need where you live. Some will have physical needs, but others who look fine on the outside still have spiritual needs on the inside.

Stop and look around your community with eyes of compassion. Look at the rich and the poor, and see their spiritual needs. Then do something about those needs.

Praise God for healing your spiritual needs by guiding you to Jesus. Thank him for the opportunity you had on your mission trip to help others who had obvious needs. Then pray that God will help you to see people in your own community whose needs may or may not be obvious and to help you show compassion to them.

My Reflection

My Reflection

HONESTY —
A HOLY POLICY

by Lindsey Miller

Growing up, my sister and I were all about pulling pranks. We were especially bent on tricking one particular lady in our church. Each week we offered to bring her coffee. While this small deed appeared to be a nice gesture, we had ulterior motives.

Once we gained her trust, we decided it was time to play a little joke on her. After filling her cup with coffee, we added sugar, salt, pepper, creamer, and any other condiments that we could find in the kitchen. We took her the cup, walked away, and watched for her reaction.

As planned, she was disgusted by what she drank. And we were proud to have deceived her!

The next Sunday we were rewarded for our dishonesty. Our prank victim decided that she would call a truce by bringing us a surprise. She revealed a plate of Twinkies just for us. We were thrilled!

With no hesitation, we quickly began devouring the treats. But we realized that something wasn't quite right. We were aware of a familiar, but unwelcome, taste in our mouths. Our friend began to laugh as she explained that she had removed the cream from the Twinkies and had replaced it with toothpaste. (To this day, I have not been able to eat a Twinkie.) Our deceit was matched, and we learned our lesson.

HONESTY LEADS TO HOLINESS

As Christians, our goal is to become more and more like God while living out his eternal purposes for his kingdom. God tells us, "Be holy because I, the LORD your God, am holy" (Leviticus 19:2).

If we are to accomplish this goal, we must first look at what God is like. And one thing we discover about God is that he does not lie. You can find evidence of this in Titus 1:2 and Hebrews 6:18. Why doesn't God lie? Because he is a holy and just God. To become more and more like God, we must live honest and holy lives.

Throughout the Old Testament, God gave his people Israel requirements for their holiness, and one of those requirements was honesty. In Deuteronomy 25:15, 16 God told his people to use honest scales in business transactions because he hates dishonesty.

HONESTY IS EXPECTED

Actually, if we really look at things, being honest it not just a nice goal we should have.

Rather, when we call ourselves followers of God, we are *expected* to be honest—it's a requirement!

Paul reminded the people of Colosse about the transformation that automatically follows when people choose to live as children of God—they are no longer like the world. Therefore, when we put off the old self and put on the new self, honesty is part of the package (Colossians 3:9, 10).

The thing is, the practice of living honestly and speaking the truth doesn't just benefit individuals—it benefits the entire community of believers, "for we are all members of one body" (Ephesians 4:25). Because we have been saved by the blood of Christ, we are to live together as a body of believers made alive through Christ. A lot of damage is done to the body if one part is full of lies.

HONESTY BRINGS UNITY

You just spent some time on a mission trip, serving alongside fellow members of Christ's body of believers. How honest were you during your trip? How did your honesty contribute to (or your dishonesty hinder) the unity of the team?

Now that you are home from your mission trip, you are rejoining the local body of believers at your church. Just like on your mission trip, being a unified team of believers is necessary in order to make a difference in your community. People who are not Christians will evaluate the message of Jesus based on the character of the Christians they meet. If you are an honest member of the body of Christ, you will draw others to the Lord.

God is truth. All the other world religions are false. By living in truth we are not only doing what he wants, we are living illustrations that his way is the true way.

Continue to be part of God's kingdom work now that you are back home. Begin by living an honest life—it's part of striving to be holy as God is holy.

Spend some time honestly evaluating your honesty. Confess the areas of your life where you need to put off falsehood and begin to speak truthfully. Pray that God will use your words of truth to demonstrate his holiness to the world.

My Reflection

My Reflection

MADE WORTHY

by Johnathan Mast

During spring break of 2002, I had the opportunity to lead my first trip to Casas Por Cristo in Mexico. Our goal, besides to spread the love of Jesus, was to build a house for a family who was homeless.

During that week our work site was blessed by a young man named Eddie. He was in elementary school, probably in third or fourth grade. Eddie came by our work site each day after school and helped us a little. But he made it his primary job to distract us and make fun of us . . . a lot! In the three days we worked on the house, we became surprisingly close to Eddie, and he seemed to have a good time around our team.

On Thursday afternoon we completed the house and presented it to the family. After loading up all the tools, we began walking toward our vehicle. As we got closer to the van, I saw Eddie standing by the doors, crying. He was upset because he knew we were leaving and he'd probably never see us again.

Eddie hugged every member of our team and begged us not to leave. I felt unworthy to have been loved so much by him. The Casas missionary said, "Eddie has seen this before. He is old enough to know that groups always come, but they never stay."

Those words made an impression on my heart. Eddie had seen many short-term mission trips, but he needed someone to stay and show him his worthiness found in Jesus.

The world is filled with people just like Eddie who need to be told the life-changing message of Jesus. We need to go to the ends of the earth and STAY. God has made us worthy by his Son, Jesus, and we are called to surrender and live a life worthy of him.

UNDESERVING

Was there a time on your mission trip when you felt unworthy to serve the people you were helping? We have all felt failure and a sense of unworthiness. And it's true that we don't deserve any honor or glory. Only God does (Revelation 4:11; Revelation 5:12).

But as Christians, we have a calling to serve God, and we need to live up to that calling (Ephesians 4:1). To live a life worthy of your calling means that you give God complete control of your life and you strive to please him in your attitude and actions.

If we seek God's wisdom and his will, we will indeed live worthy lives (Colossians 1:10).

STAY

You left one mission field, but you have come home to another mission field. Around you are people like Eddie who need to see someone stay and live out the message of Jesus.

No matter where you end up in the future—in your own hometown, across the country, or in a foreign land—be open to staying put when the Lord is nudging you to. And as you stay, allow God to make your life worthy of his calling. Surrender your attitude, actions, and future at the very feet of Jesus, and tell others about the grace he offers to undeserving people.

Praise God for loving you just as you are and for sending his Son to die so that you could be made worthy of Heaven. Commit your future to him. Ask him where he wants you to stay (or go!) in order to be used by him to touch the lives of those around you.

My Reflection

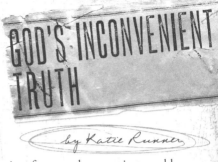

GOD'S INCONVENIENT TRUTH

by Katie Runner

We live in a fast-paced, convenient world.

Fast-food chains push to get our food to us in less than five minutes. Commercials flash a dozen images before us in a matter of seconds. Web cams allow quick access to see and talk with someone who is miles away. Songs can be downloaded to our MP3 players and into our listening ears within minutes.

Our fast-paced world teaches us to move quickly and accomplish more. But maybe there should be something to slow us down.

As believers in Christ, we do not look to our own interest but to the interests of others. The convenience of our world can sometimes create the monster of me-ism. We begin to think that this life is about ourselves.

When we are so busy getting the latest electronic gadget, checking our MySpace, and working on our accomplishments at school or work or on the sports field, we create little time to stop and look at the people around us. After all, this would use up our precious time.

Who has time to spend looking for needs other people might have? That's inconvenient. However, Jesus is asking us to inconvenience ourselves.

Maybe convenience is not all it is cracked up to be. Maybe by striving for convenience, we miss out on the moments God has placed before us, the divine moments of connection with his people.

EVERYDAY LIFESTYLE

You recently returned from a mission trip. While you were away, it may have been a great time-out from the fast pace of your life. But now that you're back, will you return to old habits, or are you ready to be inconvenienced in your everyday life for the sake of others?

You took time to notice other people while you were serving on your trip. Do you take time to see the people around you in your own community for who they really are—fellow human beings created in the image of our God? There is no unimportant person made in God's image, and there is no one we should consider as less than ourselves.

If you look in the Bible at Paul's life, you learn he lived a lifestyle of inconvenience for God's kingdom. He was ready to step out and tell others about Jesus whenever he was needed.

Read about some of Paul's experiences in 2 Corinthians 11:24-28. Imagine being beaten with rods or shipwrecked or going without sleep, food, or clothes. Paul suffered immensely for the sake of following Christ. Do you think this was convenient for him? I don't think so! However, he continued to be available whenever God needed him. Paul challenges us to do the same (Colossians 4:2-6).

PAUL'S CHALLENGES

Take some time to think through two of the challenges from Paul in this Colossians passage:

1. "Devote yourselves to prayer, being watchful and thankful" (v. 2).

As you go through the day today, be mindful of how you can pray. As you see a need, instead of passing by it, pray for the person in need and be willing to respond to that need. Pray for your heart, that you will continue to understand what serving others and giving to others is all about.

2. "Be wise in the way you act toward outsiders; make the most of every opportunity. Let your conversation be always full of grace, seasoned with salt, so that you may know how to answer everyone" (vv. 5, 6).

Most things that are good take preparation. A good meal takes preparation time in the kitchen. A good grade on a test means time spent studying beforehand. Preparation for each day as followers of Christ involves knowing God better so that we are ready for every opportunity he brings our way. Some of the ways we can prepare are by studying his Word, telling him what is on our hearts, and talking with others about what God is doing.

Be ready to step out and serve, even when it is inconvenient to you. Ask God to give you wisdom as you talk with people today. Ask him to make you ready whenever he needs you.

my Reflection

FOR SUCH A TIME AS THIS

by Lindsey Miller

It was the fall of my junior year of high school. You know what that means—football season!! Every Friday night, we gathered to cheer and encourage our school's football team. This particular Friday night, I was working in the concession stand to help raise money for our junior class. As the game was about to start, one of the cheerleaders approached me. She desperately began to explain that the person who usually wore the school mascot costume was sick and couldn't make the game; they needed a replacement.

She, of course, made it sound like a life-and-death situation: the game wouldn't be

the same without the mascot. I jumped at
the opportunity. I knew nothing about the
cheers, the dances, or the moves. But they
needed someone to get in that tiger suit, and I
knew I was just the person to do it!

The first half went well. I managed to
throw my arms around, dance a little, and
even attempt a couple of toe-touches. I was
pretty proud. After the halftime show, I came
back out with the cheerleaders and continued
to enjoy my role as the tiger. No one could
actually see my face, so I had a great time
making an absolute fool of myself.

Between the third and fourth quarters,
I heard a few twelve-year-old boys calling me.
Being the energetic and proud mascot I was,
I quickly ran over to chat with them. They
asked me questions about my life as a tiger,
and I tried my hardest to be playful. When
the fourth quarter was about to start, I turned

to join my cheerleader buddies. However, I was quickly jerked back.

While two of the boys had distracted me, a third boy had managed to tie my tiger tail to the fence without my knowing it! I was stuck! The boys busted out in laughter, knowing their trick had been successful. I quickly raised my tiger head and removed my tiger paws so I could free myself from the fence. As I lifted my tiger head, a father and daughter walked by. A distraught look came over the little girl's face as she started to cry and said to her father, "Daddy!! The tiger ate a girl!"

FIT FOR A QUEEN

We are all given opportunities. And some opportunities include making fools of ourselves as school mascots who traumatize young children! Recently, you were given the opportunity to make a difference in people's lives through your service on a mission trip. And now you have the opportunity to continue to make a difference in God's kingdom in the way you choose to live your life back at home.

In the Old Testament, we read that Esther was given an incredible opportunity, and she had to decide whether she would be a part of God's plan or not. The events in the book of Esther occurred while Israel was in exile and the Israelites were under the authority of Persia.

In Esther 1, we read that Persia's King Xerxes was hosting a banquet for his military leaders, princes, and nobles, showing off his kingdom and power. At the end of the banquet, he wanted to show off his wife, Queen Vashti, to the banquet guests. However, the queen refused his request to make an appearance. This made King Xerxes very angry, and he issued a decree that she could never enter his presence again, thus taking away her royal position.

After some time passed, the king decided to find someone else to replace the queen. Take a few minutes to read Esther 2:1-18. Esther, a young Jewish woman, was brought in with the other women to "try out" for the queen job. Because of her beauty, she stood out above the other women and won the respect of the king. Esther became the new queen.

A RISK WORTH TAKING

Check out what happened next (3:1-6). Haman, one of the king's nobles, hated Mordecai, Esther's cousin who had adopted her. Mordecai refused to bow down and honor Haman. This made Haman so angry that he began to look for a way to get rid of

Mordecai—and all the Jewish people! Haman convinced the king that the Jewish people were evil. The Jewish people were about to be destroyed (3:8-15).

Mordecai learned of Haman's plan, and he knew that the only person able to save the Jewish people from this potential genocide was Esther. Mordecai asked Esther to go into the presence of the king and plead with him to save her people.

There were some small problems though. First, the king didn't know Esther was Jewish (2:20). Second, no one was allowed in the presence of the king, including the queen, without first being summoned by him (4:11). For her to waltz into the king's court on behalf of her people could cost Esther her life.

But Mordecai told Esther, "Do not think that because you are in the king's house you alone of all the Jews will escape.

For if you remain silent at this time, relief and deliverance for the Jews will arise from another place, but you and your father's family will perish. And who knows but that you have come to royal position for such a time as this?" (4:13, 14).

Mordecai knew that God was going to save his people somehow, and he also knew that God was giving Esther the opportunity to be a part of his plan. Esther had Mordecai and the Jewish people fast for her (4:15-17). Then she went into the king's presence.

The king was pleased with her and allowed her to enter (5:1-3). Through a series of banquets, Esther got around to presenting her huge request. Esther revealed to the king that she was a Jew and begged him to save her people. The king honored her request (7:1-6). When the king discovered Haman's evil intentions behind the plan of killing the

Jews, he ordered Haman to be hung on the very gallows built to murder Mordecai (7:10). Ironic, huh?

OPPORTUNITY IS KNOCKING

Esther was given the opportunity to be used by God to save her people. She was willing to risk her life to do the right thing. Put yourself in Esther's shoes. Would you have done what she did? Would you have taken a stand, even though it included huge risks?

God uses his people to bring about his work. Mordecai told Esther that she was in a royal position "for such a time as this." God was moving, and Esther needed to get involved in his work. She wasn't a queen just so she could be comfortable. She was a queen so she could save God's people.

God created you with talents, dreams, and abilities, and he wants you to use those gifts to glorify him so others will be drawn to him. When you always do your best, other people will be drawn to Jesus and his goodness and grace. You aren't a student just so you can get good grades. You don't play basketball just so you can win a bunch of games. You don't play the trumpet just so you can perform cool songs. God has put you in your particular position to increase his kingdom. Isn't that an incredible privilege?

Look around you. How is God moving in your community? What does he want you to do to get on board? What risks is he calling you to take for him? What changes do you need to make in your life in order to be fully serving him?

Thank God for the opportunities he gave you on your mission trip to reach people for his kingdom. Then commit to serve him with the same enthusiasm in the opportunities he has for you here at home.

My Reflection

_____

_____

_____

_____

_____

_____

_____

_____

_____

_____

_____

_____

_____

_____

_____

_____

_____

EYES WIDE OPEN

by Matt Gilchrist

Today we're going to read a passage of Scripture from Acts 16. I love the way this story begins: "Once when we were going . . ." (v. 16). It sounds like something you would hear in the cafeteria or when you and your friends start telling stories to one-up each other. "Oh yeah? Well, I remember the time when . . ." Although Luke, the author, wasn't trying to one-up anyone, I find his story conversational as we get to peek in on an incredible experience.

TRAGEDY STRIKES

Paul and Silas, along with Luke and some others, were going to a place of prayer and were met by a slave girl who was possessed by a demon. They did not seek out this girl; they already had a full schedule!

The girl kept shouting at them for days, and finally Paul was so troubled that he cast the demon out of her (vv. 17, 18). Although this was good for the girl, it didn't make her owners happy because the spirit inside the girl had been making them money. So the owners had Paul and Silas thrown in jail (v. 19). Actually, it was a lot worse than that—they were stripped and beaten as well (vv. 22, 23).

Let's pause right there. Paul and Silas had been beaten and were in chains in prison. In my mind this seems like a natural place to end the story. But just when I think the story is ending, God is getting ready to step in. . . .

TURNING POINT

A pivotal moment happened between verses 24 and 25. It's a moment between tragedy and purpose. After any horrible situation occurs, people can get discouraged and give up. But Paul and Silas chose to take their persecution and be used by God through it.

So in verse 25, we read that, even though Paul and Silas had been beaten and chained, they were praying and singing hymns. These guys really understood that God could use them wherever they were, even in prison!

Now read verses 26-34. God miraculously worked through an earthquake, and Paul and Silas were present to tell their jailer about the salvation of Jesus. Right time, right place! In the end, the jailer and his entire family were led into a relationship with God. Even crazier than that, the jailer

invited them into his home to eat an
amazing meal with his family!

God can take any situation and change
it into something amazing. Your choice is
whether you are willing to be used by God
even in the toughest of circumstances.

AN ORDINARY MISSION FIELD

We may expect God to use us during
obvious times like a mission trip, but God is
working all the time. One of our big jobs as
Christians is to have our eyes open and notice
wherever God might want to use us to change
the world. That means he may be waiting to
use you in places that don't seem exciting to
you, such as the house you grew up in, the
school you're forced to attend, or the job you
begrudgingly go to every day. Although these
locations may not necessarily be negative
for you, they may seem average or ordinary

because you are there all the time. Yet where you are right now is where God has put you. That's your mission field.

Often we look too far ahead as to how we're going to serve God "someday"—down the road, when we're older, richer, etc. But let's not have such big dreams about the future that we miss out on opportunities right now.

Paul and Silas did not start that eventful day with a plan to run into a possessed slave girl, anger her owners, get stripped and beaten and thrown in jail, cause an earthquake, convert the jailer and his entire family, and then end with dinner at the jailer's house. That happened to be God's plan, and Paul and Silas, living with a heart for Jesus, got to be a part of it.

PEOPLE, PLACES, AND THINGS

What might happen if you lived your life with your eyes wide open, looking for opportunities God might put before you? Can you think of an occasion when you missed a chance to be a part of God's plan?

Take some time to consider the people you hang out with, the places you go, and the ways God might use you in your daily routine. Also think of hard times you have gone through that God might be able to turn into good by connecting you with others who are hurting. Pray about the people, places, and things that come to mind.

I challenge you to keep your eyes wide open and discover where God might have a job for you to do.

My Reflection

My Reflection

BE AN ENCOURAGER

by Ben Hedger

Do you often write letters? Maybe you write a pen pal or friend from church camp. Maybe your mom makes you write thank-you notes to your relatives for all your Christmas presents. When's the last time you wrote an old-fashioned letter using pen and paper? Now people text or send e-mail letters. Whatever method you use to compose your letters, the important thing is that the people you send them to feel encouraged when they read your notes.

In the New Testament, Paul wrote a couple of letters to his friend Timothy to encourage Timothy in the work that he was doing.

Paul had been a partner and mentor in young Timothy's ministry. Paul knew that the purpose for his life was to preach about Christ, and he brought Timothy along to do the same. Timothy encountered opposition to his ministry and probably was discouraged. Paul wanted to encourage Timothy to refocus and remember that it was God himself who had called them to the task of testifying about Christ.

Paul used the first portion of his second letter to remind Timothy of his foundation of faith (2 Timothy 1:3-6). Paul also reminded Timothy about how God had equipped them both with a spirit of power, love, and self-discipline (v. 7).

ENDURANCE

You need to have endurance to run a marathon, ride in the Tour de France, or compete in a triathlon event. Any of these competitions would require all the energy you could put forth.

In the Old Testament, Jeremiah needed endurance and energy for his ministry as well. As a prophet of God, Jeremiah's purpose was to share God's Word. In his case this meant warning the people of coming judgment because they kept worshiping false gods in addition to the true God. He spoke gloomy messages in a dismal time.

Read through Jeremiah sometime to see God's call on Jeremiah's life, how Jeremiah longed for the people to turn back to God, and the many different ways Jeremiah sent messages to God's people. Jeremiah had to endure physical injury, apathetic listeners, and unrepentant hearts. Jeremiah warned king after king, but they continued to lead the people away from God. Yet Jeremiah loved the people just as God loved them, and he continued to preach to and weep for them.

Because he endured so much and cared so deeply, Jeremiah was labeled the Weeping Prophet. Yet in spite of his difficult work, he was determined to fulfill the task God had put before him.

YOUR OWN ENCOURAGEMENT MINISTRY

Timothy and Jeremiah had something in common: they had tough opposition in their ministries. Each needed encouragement to endure the ministries God had for them to do.

Think of the missionaries and organizations you just worked with on your mission trip. Surely they go through discouraging times in their ministries, just as Timothy and Jeremiah did. Be like Paul and write an encouragement letter to them.

In your letter, tell them what a blessing it was to get a glimpse of what they do every day. Thank them for the opportunity you had to serve alongside them. Tell them what you learned from the experience. Then tell them what a great job they are doing and how many lives you're sure God is using them to reach. Challenge them to endure the hard times they face.

Make it a practice to write letters on a regular basis in order to encourage fellow Christians in their ministries. Don't forget all the missionaries your church supports as well as your congregation's ministers, Sunday school teachers, and other volunteers. Also encourage your friends who may be struggling through hard times—challenge them to endure in their walks with Jesus.

As you write, pray for each person, asking God to give you words they need to hear and asking God to be by their sides to give them strength.

My Reflection

My Reflection

_____

_____

_____

_____

_____

_____

_____

_____

_____

_____

_____

_____

_____

_____

_____

_____

_____

LOVE YOUR NEIGHBOR

by Matt Gilchrist

When I look back on my childhood, I recall that I had quite an assortment of neighbors. Some were good, and some were just plain scary. A quick summary of my neighbors: an alcoholic, chain-smoking heart doctor; a scary old lady; a single mom; an alcoholic dad who beat his children on a regular basis, usually in the front yard; a couple living an alternative lifestyle; a Wiccan witch; and a schoolteacher.

At first glance, this would not make up the traditional list of healthy friendships for a kid growing up in a Christian home. (OK, I apologize to any schoolteachers!) Now as a father, I would not want these people hanging around my children. You could even go so far as to say that my childhood neighborhood was its own diverse mission field.

But thinking back, I don't remember much interaction with most of my neighbors. I simply ignored them or stayed away from them. At times they were tolerated, and other than the day one of them accidentally hit me with his car, I don't think I ever spoke with them. Most of the time I was too engaged in what I was doing.

Take a minute to think about the neighbors you had when you were growing up. What relationship did you have with them?

Enter Jesus' words found in Matthew 22:39: "Love your neighbor as yourself." How do you love yourself? Why is it easier to love ourselves more than others? If you were to love and care for your neighbor the way you do yourself, what would that look like?

WHO IS YOUR NEIGHBOR?

There is another passage of Scripture where this challenge to love your neighbor appears. Take a minute to read this account in Luke 10:25-37.

For most of us, the Parable of the Good Samaritan is a familiar story. Its characters are known, its layout comfortable, and its ending predictable. But look again at the question by the expert of the law that prompted the story: "He wanted to justify himself, so he asked Jesus, 'And who is my neighbor?'" (v. 29).

The man seemed to want some clear definitions, perhaps to let him know which people he had to love and which ones he could pass by without feeling guilty. Maybe he wanted to determine how much he could do to earn "credit" in God's eyes.

Following the telling of the parable, Jesus asked a question of this expert in the law. "'Which of these three do you think was a neighbor to the man who fell into the hands of robbers?' The expert in the law replied, 'The one who had mercy on him.' Jesus told him, 'Go and do likewise'" (vv. 36, 37).

The man got his answer from Jesus— God considered anyone and everyone to be the man's neighbor. The same goes for us. The call of Christ is to love our neighbors— that means not just the people who live by us, but anyone and everyone we encounter.

It is our mission in life, not just on a mission trip, to notice those around us, to love them, to know them, and to offer care and hope. Right now your eyes are opened. You spent time on your mission trip in a setting that made you more aware of the things happening around you and more willing to respond to the needs you saw. Perhaps you were more selfless than normal. How are you making sure this doesn't change now that you've returned home?

HOW WILL YOU LOVE?

List your neighbors—at home, at school, at work, at church, etc. Then ask God to show you some ways you can love the neighbors in these places.

It's easy to love the neighbors who are like us, but what obstacles will you have to overcome to love neighbors who aren't like you? How would *you* love the alcoholic heart doctor, the Wiccan, or—horrors—the schoolteacher!

What is your biggest challenge to overcome in loving your neighbors? (And while you're at it, what obstacles do you think others have had to overcome to love you?) How can you begin overcoming that obstacle today?

Start by showing mercy to everyone you come in contact with today. That might mean offering an encouraging word, a smile, or simply looking someone in the eye. How could those simple acts begin to change others' lives and your own?

Take some time to thank God for showing you mercy. Thank him for loving you despite the fact that you are so different from him and don't deserve his love. Ask him to help you love others as you love yourself.

My Reflection

CHANGE OF ADDRESS

by Dorothy Eunson

"Where are ya from?" Were you asked that question anytime on your mission trip? It was easy to answer: "Johnson City, Tennessee" or "Salem, Missouri" or "Lock Haven, Pennsylvania." Your family, friends, school, and church are there. Things and people in that town are familiar and comfortable, even dear to you. It's home.

Perhaps you have left home for college. Did you get homesick at first? How does it feel to have two homes now?

In the future, would you be willing to consider making a major change of physical address, away from all that is familiar, for the sake of Christ? Let's study about a man who did and find out what empowered him to do so.

A FOREIGN LAND

Read Genesis 12:1-4 and Hebrews 11:8-16. At age seventy-five, Abraham (or actually Abram, before his name change) left his country, his kinsmen, and his father's home for an unknown destination. He did it in obedience to a God he trusted.

Yes, the promises of prosperity and protection were given. But without faith in God, Abraham might have refused to begin the journey, especially since he didn't even know where he was going (Hebrews 11:8).

What lifestyle did Abraham follow in the new land? Hebrews 11:9 says he lived as "a stranger in a foreign country."

ALIENS AND STRANGERS

Verse 13 says that Abraham and all the people of faith mentioned in Hebrews 11 openly "admitted that they were aliens and strangers on earth." They knew the language and the customs, but in many ways they did not belong because they followed God's ways—and his standards were far above those of the society around them. They were missionaries.

What principles did these "aliens" follow?

1. They did not keep "thinking of the country they had left" (v. 15). That is hard to do when you are in a new place with detestable customs and the people you have always loved are far away! How was it possible?

2. Their eyes were on the goal of a city with permanent foundations, a heavenly

home with God (v. 16). That was more real and compelling than their temporary homes on earth.

And how did God view their attitudes? God was "not ashamed to be called their God" (v. 16). Fantastic!

GLORIOUS RESULTS

What was the result of Abraham's faith and willingness to leave his original home? His descendants became the nation of Israel with its own homeland. Jesus Christ, the Savior of the world, was born into that nation. And through Jesus, people of all nations are invited to have a relationship with God. All of us who choose Jesus become spiritual descendants of Abraham, the man who lived as a stranger in a strange land.

Who had the greatest change of address of all? Jesus Christ! He willingly left the glories of Heaven, "made himself nothing," took the nature of a servant, and came to earth in human likeness. He was humble and was obedient even to his death on the cross. His death and resurrection opened the way to salvation for all humankind (Philippians 2:5-11).

MY CHANGE OF ADDRESS

For thirty-eight years Ghana has been my home. When I first came to Ghana to work with Ghana Christian College, I had not been here before; in fact, I had never been out of the United States. I knew no one here except through correspondence, and I'd only just begun to know the other missionaries I met on the plane ride over. I felt, however, that at last I was where God wanted me to be.

That's not to ignore the fact that at times it has been very difficult. I remember being a little homesick my first Christmas. And one time, just before I took a furlough, I even said I was never coming back. But my visit in the States refreshed me, and back I came!

I am still a foreigner here and always will be, but I live, work, and worship among my Ghanian brothers and sisters. Good memories and bad, victories and defeats—they are all part of a lifetime I would not exchange for any other. It has been a privilege to serve God, serve others, and grow in my faith in a foreign country and culture.

Soon I will face another change of address—retirement to the United States, particular destination unknown. I am trusting God to lead me to the place I can afford and the place I can best serve him. I know from experience that I can serve him anywhere; so I'm a little nervous—but not afraid—about where he might decide to send me.

WILL YOU GO?

Abraham did it. Jesus did it. I've done it—as have thousands of others like me. Can you face a different climate, different language, different money, different laws, different driving habits, different religions, different worldviews, and many different customs for the sake of spreading the gospel of Christ around the world?

Even if you do not become a missionary in the traditional sense, these principles will help you adjust anywhere and be a light shining in the darkness. Are you ready to change your address?

Will you pray about this? Use this prayer if you want:

"God, you are the Lord of the universe. May your name be praised! 'I can never escape from your Spirit! I can never get away from your presence! If I go up to heaven, you are there; if I go down to the grave, you are there. If I ride the wings of the morning, if I dwell by the farthest oceans, even there your hand will guide me, and your strength will support me' (Psalm 139:7-10, *NLT*).

"Help me to remember your promise never to leave me or abandon me (Hebrews 13:5). Help me to fix my eyes on Jesus, 'the author and perfecter of [my] faith' (Hebrews 12:2). Fill me with courage to follow your leading anywhere on earth for your sake. Help me to be like Jesus, in whose name I pray. Amen."

My Reflection

My Reflection

STRENGTH FOR A LIFETIME

by Katie Runner

Years ago, when people left to work as missionaries overseas, some packed their clothes and belongings in coffins, knowing they were probably not going to return to their homeland. They said good-bye to friends and family, realizing that they would most likely be buried in the country where they were going to live.

They knew their lives could be cut short by life-threatening illnesses or lack of medical care and medicines. They also understood that they would be pouring their entire lives into the people they were going to serve. Knowing all this, they went anyway, relying on the strength of God.

I look at examples like this and wonder, *Do I know anything about commitment?*

Today we have opportunities to serve God cross-culturally for one week, two weeks, six weeks, one year . . . These are great moments that help us see another way of life and grow in an understanding of God's heart for all people. However, after we complete our time, we can easily return to so-called normal life, if we choose. We can go back to living our lives of comfort, spending as much money as we want on things we do not need, squandering countless hours online or in front of the TV, doing what feels best for each of us. I am guilty of it too. Then there are those moments when I ask myself again, *Do I know anything about commitment?*

TO THE ENDS OF THE EARTH

Think about being committed for a

lifetime. From the beginning of creation, God has been calling all people to himself, desiring to make himself known to the nations. And you know what? He has chosen to let us have a part in this task! Isn't that exciting?

In Acts Jesus called the first church to reach Jerusalem, Judea, Samaria, and the ends of the earth (Acts 1:8). Jesus asked the first believers to touch those places with the glory of Christ to spread God's kingdom! This included people who lived right next door, along with those very far away. God wanted it to be known that his heart is for all people.

This same truth is for us today because God desires to use us to reach all people, wherever they are located. God wants us to be living out his mission of extending the love of Christ to everyone.

As you served cross-culturally on your mission trip, what did you learn? Even though you have returned home and are back into the familiar routine, continue to ask God, "How can I be a part of your work?" Consider taking specific steps to commit to God's mission where you are right now.

Maybe your trip challenged you begin a ministry in your city. Maybe you need to finally take a step in talking with your friend at school about your relationship with Christ. Maybe God is challenging you to pray for an unreached people group. Maybe you realized you want to prepare to go into full-time missionary work.

Whatever the task, it will not be unimportant! God is a God of accomplishing what seems impossible! Remember that God has equipped you (or will) for everything he desires for you to do. He is the one who gives us the strength we need. We just need to be willing—willing to serve, in whatever way he desires, for a lifetime.

Let's keep a few things in mind:

1. God's strength is your strength. You are not alone. In your weakness, God's strength is showcased. The Lord says, "My grace is sufficient for you, for my power is made perfect in weakness" (2 Corinthians 12:9).

When we do something completely new, we will likely feel incapable and inadequate. On your mission trip, you may have felt weak as you have tried to communicate either in a different language or in a different cultural context. It is through times like these that we understand and see God's power at work, despite our mistakes or weaknesses. We have to rely on him and not on our own power.

I have never felt weaker than when I was trying to learn a language and build relationships in a country that was completely new to me. I also have never seen God's power at work more than in those times of my weakness; he showed himself faithful.

2. God has appointed you. The moment you committed your life to God, he made you a part of his mission. He asks all followers to have the same heart as he because he "wants everyone to be saved and to understand the truth" (1 Timothy 2:4, *NLT*).

As a believer in Christ, you have been specially commissioned to be a part of bringing others into his kingdom. When you don't understand what is happening or you feel you are experiencing difficulty after difficulty, know that God has chosen you, he wants to use you in his work—and he knows what he's doing!

3. God is full of grace. Paul, who called himself the worst of sinners, understood God's grace. Paul did not deserve God's

forgiveness after all he had done (persecuting the church and destroying God's work), but God corrected Paul and used him for kingdom work (1 Timothy 1:12-14).

We also do not deserve God's forgiveness and grace. Yet God has given us a relationship with him. He essentially has said, "Even though you have done nothing to deserve forgiveness, I will forgive you through my Son." Because God has been full of grace toward us, we must be full of grace toward others. As you follow the Lord's lead today, strive to treat others with that same grace.

A LIFETIME COMMITMENT

When, or how, did you feel weak on your mission trip? How did you see God's strength and power revealed through that weakness? How have you felt weak since you returned home? What is one way you can focus on carrying out God's mission as you live out your daily routine?

Your mission trip is over, but your commitment to God's kingdom continues. What he has begun in your heart needs to spur you on to serve him for the rest of your life, no matter where he leads you or what he asks of you.

Thank God for doing impossible things. Thank him for allowing you to anticipate and experience a mission trip that placed you in a culture different from your own. Also thank him for time to reflect on all he taught you.

Seek ways that you can continue to be a part of God's mission to tell all people about his salvation through Jesus. Commit to being God's ambassador in your own community and wherever he leads you in the future. Trust God for strength, and live for his glory.

my Reflection

My Reflection